Healing Hands

The Story of
Dr. Benjamin Carson

by Karen Kellaher

SCHOLASTIC INC.

New York Toronto London Auckland Sydney
Mexico City New Delhi Hong Kong Buenos Aires

Cover Photo Credits:
Courtesy Johns Hopkins Children's Center

3 4 5 6 7 8 9 10   08   12 11 10 09 08 07 06 05 04

Contents

Dr. Ben Carson performs high-risk brain surgeries. His work has made him famous around the world.

Introduction

The year is 1966. The place is Detroit, Michigan. Ben Carson is an angry teenager. He stands with a knife in his hand. He has just tried to stab his friend over a silly disagreement. Ben is horrified at what he has done. Thankful that his friend is unhurt, he runs home.

Fast forward to today. The angry teen is now an adult. Again he stands with a sharp blade in his hand. Only this time, he is using it to save someone. A young girl has a deadly tumor on her brain. Dr. Ben Carson must open the girl's skull. Then he will slice into the girl's brain to remove the lump.

Inside the operating room, tension fills the air. Machines hum and beep. Outside the room, the girl's parents wait for news. They know that their daughter's life is in the doctor's hands.

This is a true story. Dr. Benjamin Carson is one

of the world's best pediatric neurosurgeons. A neurosurgeon is a doctor who operates on people's brains. A pediatric neurosurgeon operates on children. Dr. Carson works at Johns Hopkins Hospital in Baltimore, Maryland. Every year, he performs brain surgery on hundreds of sick kids. People from all around the world come to him for treatment.

Dr. Carson has a big title. He is the chief of pediatric neurosurgery at the hospital. That means he is in charge of the whole department. He is the youngest doctor and the first African American to hold this important position.

Dr. Carson dreamed of becoming a doctor when he was just a kid. But the road to success was not easy. Growing up, Ben Carson faced all kinds of problems. His family was poor. He dealt with racism. He struggled with bad grades. He had a bad temper. Sometimes it looked like he would never achieve his dream.

1 Broken Home, Broken Heart

"I want to be a doctor!"

That's what Ben Carson told his family one day in 1959. He was only eight years old. But he was sure. The Carsons had just been to church. The pastor had told a story. It made Ben shiver with excitement. The story was about a doctor who saved lives in a dangerous, far-off land. Ben thought that being a doctor sounded like an adventure. He decided then and there on a career in medicine.

Ben had no idea how hard it would be to reach his goal. For starters, his family did not have much money. The Carsons lived in a tiny house in Detroit, Michigan. They barely had enough money to pay the bills. His dad worked long hours in a car factory. But he did not earn a lot. His mom had left school after the third grade. She had few job skills.

Later that year, things went from bad to worse. Ben's mom, Sonya, discovered that her husband had been telling lies. He had another wife and family in another part of the city. After an argument, Ben's dad left home. Sonya had a talk with Ben and his ten-year-old brother, Curtis. She explained that she and their father were getting a divorce.

Ben cried for a long time. He did not know the whole story. He thought the divorce was his fault. "Make him come back!" he begged his mom. But after a while, Ben realized that his dad was gone for good.

The divorce meant tough times for the Carsons. Without her husband's paycheck, Sonya Carson could not pay for the family's home, heat, electricity, and food. Bills began to pile up. Ben's mom also became depressed. She sometimes had to go to a hospital for treatment. At those times, friends would take care of Ben and Curtis.

After a few months, Ben's mom made a tough decision. She and her sons would move in with relatives. It would just be for a while. They would rent their house to someone else until they were back on their feet.

So off they went to Boston, Massachusetts. Ben's Aunt Jean and Uncle William welcomed the Carsons with open arms. The Averys' own children were grown up. The couple had a lot of love to share. Ben and Curtis felt safe and happy in their new home.

Outside the apartment, it was a different story. The Averys lived in one of the poorest neighborhoods in Boston. Rats and roaches scurried out of trash piles. Graffiti covered the buildings. There was a lot of crime.

Ben's mom struggled to help her family. She found work cleaning houses and babysitting. She was tired. She often worked two or three jobs at a time. By 1961, she had saved enough money to bring her sons back to Detroit.

The Carsons could not afford to move back to their old house right away. They still needed the money the renters were paying them each month. So they found a small apartment in a different neighborhood. Ben was ten years old.

Ben started fifth grade at Higgins Elementary School in Detroit. He was in for a surprise. He was way behind the other kids. In Boston, school had been pretty easy. He had not needed to study much. But in Detroit, the lessons were much harder. At report card time, Ben and his mom were shocked to see his grades:

Math: F

History: F

English: F

Ben was failing nearly every subject! His classmates teased him. They called him a dummy. Before long, Ben started to believe the nickname was true.

2 No Dummy

Ben's mom knew her son could do better. So she set new rules to help Ben turn his grades around. First, she made sure Ben and his brother studied every day. She found out that Ben didn't know the times tables. So she made him memorize them. "I only went through third grade, and I know them all the way through my twelves," she told Ben. Every night, she would drill him. "What's 4 times 5?" she would ask. "What's 10 times 12?" At first Ben did not know any of the answers. But before long, he knew them all.

Next, Sonya Carson made a new rule about television. Before, Ben and Curtis had been allowed to watch TV whenever they wanted. Now they could see only three shows each week! Mrs. Carson wanted the boys to spend time reading instead of watching TV. She told Ben and Curtis that they had to read two library books every week.

They had to write reports about the books and give the reports to their mom. Ben grumbled about the new rules. He had never read a whole book before in his life!

Ben discovered that he loved reading about new things. He especially liked books about science and nature. The more he read, the more curious he became about the world around him. Sometimes he would walk next to the train tracks. He would pick up rocks and try to name them. Other times, Ben would visit a stream in his neighborhood. He would try to identify the insects he saw in the water.

Ben's grades slowly began to go up. The F's turned into C's. Then the C's turned into A's. By the end of fifth grade, Ben was no longer at the bottom of the class. Now he was at the top!

One day, Ben's science teacher held up a shiny black rock. She asked the class what it was. Ben knew. Nobody else did. Ben recognized the rock from his library books. "That's obsidian," he said. When Ben's teacher said that he was right, the other students were amazed. They would never call him a dummy again. The same kids who had teased Ben started asking him for help.

Ben's brother, Curtis, was doing well in school, too. They were grateful to their mom for making them read and write. But there was a secret that they would not learn until they were adults. All that time, Mrs. Carson had never read a word of their book reports! She had left school at age eight. She had never learned to read. But that did not stop her from expecting the best from her sons.

Ben graduated from Higgins Elementary School. He moved on to Wilson Junior High and kept getting straight A's. For two years in a row, he received the school's award for best student.

But Ben also began to experience racism. Wilson Junior High was mostly white. Some of the kids and teachers could not believe that an African-American student could do so well. One day, a teacher yelled at the white students for letting a black student do better than them! Another time, Ben and his brother were threatened by a gang of white teens. The teens called Ben and Curtis racist names. They told the brothers they did not belong at Wilson.

Ben told himself that the racist teacher and teens didn't know anything. But inside, he felt hurt and angry. Those feelings sometimes got Ben into trouble. He began fighting at school. Once, he even tried to hit his mom during an argument. His brother stopped the blow. But it was a sign that Ben's temper was getting worse.

3 Taming a Bad Temper

In the middle of eighth grade, Ben's family moved again. This time, the Carsons moved back to their old house. Sonya Carson had been working hard. She had saved money. The family could finally afford to live there again.

Ben had missed his old home. He was excited to be back! But he was nervous about changing schools in the middle of the year.

Ben's new school was Hunter Junior High. Most of the students at Hunter were African American. That meant Ben did not face racism the way he used to. But some of the kids at Hunter made fun of Ben for a different reason. They saw that he earned top grades and spent a lot of time studying. They treated Ben like an outsider.

Ben wanted very badly to have friends. He decided to work at fitting in. He noticed that the popular kids had some things in common. For one thing, they all played basketball after school. So Ben started shooting hoops instead of doing homework. Some nights, he stayed out until ten o'clock. He did not care that his mother was disappointed.

Ben also noticed that the popular kids wore leather jackets and designer clothes. He had never worried about clothes before. Now he begged his mom to buy him the latest styles. "I can't wear this," he would complain. "Everyone will laugh at me." Ben's mom saved up to buy a few special things for him. But she could not afford to buy more.

Ben's plan to fit in worked. He made friends and got invited to parties. He had fun. But deep down, he was not very happy. By the end of junior high, Ben's grades had dropped. His report cards were full of C's instead of A's. And his temper had grown hotter and hotter.

One day, Ben had a close call during an argument. Ben and his friend Bob were listening to the radio. Bob did not like the song that was playing. "You call that music?" he asked Ben. Then Bob turned the dial to a different station.

Ben grew angry. Without thinking, he grabbed a camping knife from his pocket. He shoved the knife toward his friend's stomach. Ben was lucky. The knife hit Bob's belt buckle. It snapped in half. It did not cut Bob.

Ben could not believe what he had done. He ran home and locked himself in the bathroom. For hours, Ben cried and prayed. He still dreamed of being a doctor. He wanted to save people—not hurt them. But he knew his dream would never come true if he did not turn his life around. Finally, Ben made a promise to himself. His temper was out of control. He would tame it once and for all.

4 *A Bright Future*

In 1967, Ben started at Southwestern High School. He joined the school's Reserve Officer Training Corps (ROTC) program. It is a program run by the United States Armed Forces. As a member of ROTC, Ben still studied the regular subjects like math, science, English, and history. But he also took special classes to learn about leadership and military skills. He wore an ROTC uniform to school most days. He no longer had to worry about having the "right" clothes.

Ben's brother Curtis had been a member of ROTC for two years. His uniform was covered in medals. Ben was proud of Curtis. He hoped to follow in his big brother's footsteps.

Joining ROTC was good for Ben. He began studying again. His grades went back up. Like his brother, he received many awards. He earned promotion after promotion in the ROTC program.

In 1969, Ben graduated from high school with top honors. Many colleges wrote to him. They all wanted him to choose their school.

Ben had a tough time choosing. Most colleges charged a fee just to look at a student's application. Ben only had enough money for one application fee. So he settled on Yale University in Connecticut. He sent in his application and crossed his fingers. Soon there was great news. Ben did not just get into Yale. He was offered a scholarship, too!

Ben headed to college in the fall of 1969. It was harder than he expected. Yale was full of smart students. Ben had to work hard to keep getting good grades.

Ben's toughest subject was chemistry. It was an important class for students who wanted to be doctors. But Ben was doing poorly. He worried that he might fail the class. He knew he had to do well on the final exam.

Then an amazing thing happened. On the day before the big exam, Ben studied for hours. At midnight, he could not keep his eyes open. He said a prayer and fell asleep. That night, Ben had a strange dream. He dreamed that he was taking his chemistry test. One by one, he answered the questions correctly.

The next day, Ben sat down to take the exam. He could not believe his eyes. The questions were the same ones that he had seen in his dream! Ben remembered the right answers. When he got his test back, Ben saw that he had gotten a 97. It was almost a perfect score! Ben believed that his dream was God's way of helping him become a doctor.

When Ben graduated from Yale, he had the love and support of his mother (left), and Candy (right).

Courtesy Johns Hopkins Children's Center

In his third year at Yale, Ben met someone special. She was a student named Lacena Rustin. Lacena's nickname was Candy. Ben and Candy had a lot to talk about. They both loved reading books. They both listened to classical music. Before long, the two were in love.

Ben graduated from Yale in 1973. It was time for medical school. Ben decided to study medicine at the University of Michigan. It was in the state where Ben had grown up. The medical school had a policy that would save Ben money. Students from Michigan did not pay as much to go there as students from other states did. Ben was excited to start his medical training. But he was sad about one thing. Candy still had one year left at Yale. Ben knew he would miss her terribly.

5 *Ben Carson, M.D.*

At medical school, Ben studied from six in the morning until eleven at night. But he always saved a few minutes for a letter or phone call to Candy. The couple stayed close. After Candy graduated from Yale, she moved to Michigan. The couple got married. Afterward, Candy worked while Ben studied.

Soon Ben had to decide what type of doctor to become. Would he be a family doctor? Did he want to be a surgeon, who performs operations? He was not sure.

In his third year of medical school, Ben worked in many different departments of the hospital. His favorite department was neurosurgery. Neurosurgeons are doctors who operate on people's brains. They help patients with brain tumors and other problems.

Ben was fascinated with the human brain. And he was good at assisting during operations. He decided to become a neurosurgeon.

In 1977, Ben graduated from medical school. He had achieved his dream of becoming a doctor. But he still had more to learn. The next stage of his medical training was an internship. An intern works alongside more experienced doctors.

Ben was accepted into the internship program at Johns Hopkins Hospital in Baltimore, Maryland. This was a great achievement. Johns Hopkins had one of the best neurosurgery departments in the country.

During his internship, Ben learned a lot about his field. He also learned to deal with racism again. Some patients did not like the fact that Ben was African American. They would not let him examine them. And sometimes, nurses would tell Ben to push a wheelchair or clean a room. They thought Ben was an orderly. That's a person who works as a hospital helper. They were not used to seeing black doctors.

Ben ignored the prejudice he faced. Doing a

good job was what mattered to him. The internship was supposed to take two years. But Ben worked extra hard. He finished the internship in one year. His bosses were impressed.

For the next five years, Ben stayed at Johns Hopkins as a resident. A resident is a doctor who is getting advanced training in his or her special field. As a resident, Ben learned more about operating on people's brains. He began to perform operations by himself.

Ben spent a lot of time working in the hospital. But he also did research in a laboratory. He studied rabbits that had brain tumors. He wanted to learn how tumors grow. His research taught him and other doctors a lot about human brain tumors.

All that hard work paid off. In 1982, Ben got two big honors. He was named the hospital's Resident of the Year. He was also invited to be the chief resident. That put him in charge of the other neurosurgery residents at the hospital.

At the end of that year, Ben was given an exciting opportunity. A hospital in Australia was looking for a neurosurgeon. It was a year-long job.

The job would let Ben and Candy see another part of the world. Ben and Candy decided to go. They left for Australia in June of 1983.

It was a happy year for the Carsons. They joined the local Seventh-Day Adventist church. It was the same kind of church they attended back home. They made many good friends through the church. At the hospital, Ben got to treat hundreds of patients. He learned new surgical skills. And best of all, Candy gave birth to the couple's first son. They named him Murray.

Soon it was time to return to the United States. Back in Maryland, Ben got a call from his old bosses at Johns Hopkins Hospital. They wanted him to work there again. They asked him to become their chief of pediatric neurosurgery.

It was an important and challenging job. Ben would be responsible for a whole department of the hospital. But he did not have to think twice. He accepted the hospital's offer. He was just 33 years old. He became the youngest person—and the first African-American doctor—ever to hold that job.

Courtesy Johns Hopkins Children's Center

Dr Carson's medical expertise and his skill at working with children make him a great doctor. Here he paints with a three-year-old patient.

6 In the Spotlight

In 1985, Dr. Carson met a patient who would change his life. Four-year-old Maranda Francisco was having seizures. During each seizure, her whole body would shake. Little Maranda could hardly eat or talk. She would often have a hundred seizures in one day.

Maranda had an inflammation, or swelling, on one side of her brain. If the problem wasn't fixed, it would get worse. The swelling could paralyze Maranda. She would be unable to move. It could also kill her.

Maranda was from Colorado. Doctors there had tried many medications to stop the problem. But nothing had helped. Then Maranda's parents heard about Johns Hopkins. They heard that the neurosurgeons there were doing great work. They flew their daughter all the way to Maryland.

Dr. Carson knew that surgery was Maranda's only hope. He and his team would have to remove the swollen half of Maranda's brain. This type of operation is called a hemispherectomy. That's because each half of the brain is called a hemisphere.

The operation would be risky. Each part of the human brain has jobs to do. Some parts control the way we speak and hear. Some parts control the way we move. No one was sure what would happen if doctors cut out half of Maranda's brain. Would she be able to walk and talk? Dr. Carson thought so. He believed that the right half of Maranda's brain would start doing all the jobs.

The surgeons told Maranda's parents the truth. There was a chance that their daughter could die on the operating table. She could also end up with brain damage. But it was worth the risk. There was no other way to help Maranda.

Dr. Carson and his team operated on Maranda for ten hours. They removed a big chunk of Maranda's brain. Then they put the top of her skull back in place.

The operation worked! Even though half of Maranda's brain was gone, she could still talk, walk, and play. The right side of Maranda's brain began doing jobs that the left side used to do. It happened just like Dr. Carson had hoped.

Dr. Carson was not surprised that the surgery was a success. But he was surprised to see his name in the headlines the next day. Newspaper and TV reports told about the doctor who saved Maranda. Since then, Dr. Carson has performed the same operation many times.

One year later, Dr. Carson had another big case. A couple from Germany had conjoined twins who needed help. Conjoined twins are sometimes called Siamese twins. They are born with parts of their bodies connected.

The Binder twins were connected at the backs of their skulls. The babies were healthy. But unless they were separated, they would never learn to sit up, roll over, or walk.

Separating the twins was a huge challenge. Such an operation had never been done successfully. But Dr. Carson and his fellow surgeons wanted to try.

The doctors knew what had to be done. Each baby had his own brain. But there were important veins running between the two brains. Veins are the tiny tubes that carry blood through the body. Doctors would have to separate the veins carefully. They would have to give each baby the veins he needed. They would also have to make sure the twins did not lose too much blood.

Planning the surgery took months. Finally, Dr. Carson and his team started the operation. There were 70 doctors and nurses on the team.

The surgery took 22 hours! It was harder than Dr. Carson had imagined. Both babies lost a lot of blood. Their brains became swollen from the surgery. But in the end it was a success. Patrick and Benjamin Binder left the operating room as two babies. Both would be just fine.

Again, Dr. Carson found himself in the spotlight. Soon, people from all over the globe were asking him for help.

7 *A Doctor's Day*

Today, Dr. Carson is one of the most successful neurosurgeons in the world. People travel thousands of miles to have him operate on them. Every year, he performs more than 400 operations. That's three times the number of operations that most neurosurgeons perform!

Most of Dr. Carson's patients are children with brain tumors and other serious problems. Many are cases that other doctors have called hopeless. But Dr. Carson never gives up hope. He will try anything to save a patient's life. Of course, not every patient makes it. Each time a patient dies, Dr. Carson shares the family's grief.

Dr. Carson's schedule would wear most people out. He gets to the hospital by 7:30 in the morning. He spends the whole morning in the operating room. In the afternoon, he examines patients in his office and at the hospital. But that's not all. Somehow, he also finds time to run his department of the hospital and teach young doctors.

As busy as he is, Dr. Carson always makes time for his family. He and Candy have three sons: Murray, Ben Jr., and Rhoeyce. The boys are young adults now. They are very close to their parents. Dr. Carson's mom, Sonya, also lives with the family.

Dr. Carson heads home by eight or nine o'clock each night. That way, he can have time with his family. He spends weekends at home with them, too. They swim, play tennis, and enjoy board games together. They also like to read. One thing the Carsons do not do much is watch TV! Dr. Carson believes that turning off the TV helped him reach his dream. He wants the same thing for his sons.

Work and family are not the only things that bring Dr. Carson joy. His faith in God remains strong. The Carsons attend a Seventh-Day Adventist church in Spencerville, Maryland. Dr. Carson is very active in the church. He says that he could not have become a doctor without God's help.

Dr. Carson makes his family a priority. He and his sons have always been close.

Not long ago, Dr. Carson's faith was tested. In June 2002, he found out that he had cancer. Later that summer, Dr. Carson had surgery to remove the cancer. It was a success.

Dr. Carson says that the illness made him a better doctor. It taught him what it is like to be a sick patient. It helped him understand just how scared his own patients might feel. Dr. Carson uses everything he has learned to help others.

On his first day back at work after being treated for cancer, Dr. Carson is welcomed by the mother of one of his patients.

8 Think Big

Ben Carson remembers the challenges he faced when he was young. He overcame racism, poverty, violence, and low grades. Dr. Carson knows that many young people face the same problems today. He tries to help them achieve their own dreams. One way he does this is through a scholarship program. In 1994, Dr. and Mrs. Carson began helping kids in the Baltimore, Maryland, area. Each scholarship winner gets $1,000 to help pay for college. Students win the scholarships by getting good grades.

Dr. Carson also helps kids by talking about his experiences. A few times a year, crowds of students go to Johns Hopkins. They pack the hospital auditorium. They want to hear Dr. Carson's story.

Dr. Carson always gives them the same message: "Think big." He believes that thinking big is the key to success. It means never giving up on your dreams.

"Think big" is more than just a catchy phrase, though. For Dr. Carson, each letter in the phrase has a special meaning:

- **T = Talent and Time.** Dr. Carson tells students to recognize their natural talents. Perhaps they are good at math or science. Or maybe they are excellent readers. They should find what they are great at and be proud. They should use their time to help their talents grow.

- **H = Hope.** To Dr. Carson, having hope means expecting good things to happen. He tells students to look forward to their futures. He thinks that having hope can make a big difference.

- **I = Insight.** Insight is the ability to really understand something. Dr. Carson tells students that they can get insight by learning from other people's mistakes. He says kids should learn from people who have more experience than they do.

Despite his busy schedule, Dr. Carson makes time to visit schools to motivate young people.

Dr. Carson brings his message to a group of middle school students in New Mexico.

- **N = Nice.** It's not always easy to be nice. But Dr. Carson tells young people to make the effort. Being nice to others takes less energy than losing your temper! And it can stop disagreements before they get out of control.

- **K = Knowledge.** Dr. Carson believes that knowledge is power. He tells kids to learn as much as they can. When he was young, he felt terrible when classmates called him a dummy. But he felt great when the same kids asked him for help.

- **B = Books.** Books helped turn Dr. Carson's life around. He says they can do the same thing for today's young people. He encourages kids to start with short, easy books. Then they can move on to harder ones.

- **I = In-Depth Learning.** Dr. Carson wants students to keep learning—even when they are not in school. He says that many students study just to pass a test. Then they forget everything once the test is over. Dr. Carson also says that everyone learns differently. "Figure out how you learn best," he tells students. "Do you learn by reading, or by listening, or by doing?"

© CNN/Getty Images

Dr. Ben Carson worked hard to reach his goal. He hopes his story will inspire others to think big.

• **G = God.** Dr. Carson has always had a strong faith in God. He tells kids that faith helped him succeed in life.

Of course, not everyone can hear Dr. Carson speak in person. But they can still hear his amazing tale. In 1990, Dr. Carson wrote his life story. His book is called *Gifted Hands*. Since then, he has published two other books. He hopes his story will help others reach for their dreams.